WHAT YOU SHOULD KNOW ABOUT

ACCEPTING PEOPLE WHO AREN'T LIKE YOU

WHAT YOU SHOULD KNOW ABOUT

ACCEPTING PEOPLE WHO AREN'T LIKE YOU

WILLIAM L. COLEMAN

Augsburg
MINNEAPOLIS

WHAT YOU SHOULD KNOW ABOUT ACCEPTING PEOPLE
WHO AREN'T LIKE YOU

Scripture quotations unless otherwise noted are from The Holy
Bible: New International Version. Copyright © 1978 The New
York International Bible Society. Used by permission of Zonder-
van Bible Publishers.

Cover design: Bob Fuller
Interior design: Jim Brisson

Library of Congress Cataloging-in-Publication Data

Coleman, William L.
    What you should know about accepting people who aren't
like you /
    William L. Coleman.
        p.   cm.
    ISBN 0-8066-2637-2 (alk. paper) :
    1. Prejudices in children—Religious aspects—Christianity—
Juvenile literature.   2. Children—Religious life.   3. Children—
Conduct of life.   [1. Prejudices.   2. Conduct of life.
3. Christian life.]   I. Title.
BV4571.2.C594   1993
248.8'2—dc20   93-36829
                                                             CIP
                                                              AC

The paper used in this publication meets the minimum require-
ments of American National Standard for Information Sciences—
Permanence of Paper for Printed Library Materials, ANSI
Z329.48-1984.   ∞™

Manufactured in U.S.A.   AF 9-2637

97 96 95 94 93   1 2 3 4 5 6 7 8 9 10

◆ ◆ ◆ ◆ ◆

CONTENTS

CONTENTS

CONTENTS

◆ ◆ ◆ ◆ ◆

Suggestions for Adults

Thanks for showing your interest in children. If you can help one or two children be even a little less prejudiced, less afraid, less ignorant about others, you have blessed their lives. It is a terrible thing to live under the oppression of hating others. Your interest can help keep a child free from the burden of distrust and vengeance.

Prejudice is not fundamentally a child's dilemma. Most of us learn to dislike others because of what adults tell us as children. By the time we become teenagers, most of our stereotypes are firmly set. The major hope we have of accepting those who are different rests in our ability to teach the young.

Most of the wars that rage in this world began with old and unfounded prejudices. Peoples who have hated each other for hundreds of years pass that anger on to their children.

As an adult you can take a step forward to change that pattern. To help you in that task, I want to suggest how you might best use this book.

1. *Don't read the book straight through.* If your child is eager to discuss a subject right away, turn to that chapter and make it the topic of the day. Spending ten to fif-

teen minutes a day reading chapters from the book and affirming what it says, can be very helpful.

2. *Be open to questions that might occur to your child.* If you don't know, say so. Don't bluff or you could create a distrust. If possible, offer to help your child find the answer.

3. *Eventually read all the chapters.* What may not interest your child today could prove very helpful tomorrow. Later when your child meets someone he or she has read about, the situation may not seem so uncomfortable.

4. *Don't defend everyone.* You can't anyway. If a child hears of a blind person who robbed a bank, don't hurry to make up a defense for the blind person. Rather, explain that not all blind people or white people or carnival workers steal and rob. If the child sees that you will defend everyone, you will lose credibility.

5. *Admit that you have had prejudices and still do.* The eight- to twelve-year-old has prejudices and needs to know that others do too. You don't have to confess every twinge of dislike you have ever felt, but at least confess to some feelings, if even in the vaguest of terms.

6. *Include the feelings of God.* Many prejudices are heavily intertwined with bad

theology. Some of us think we are supposed to hate some people. This book should furnish a good opportunity to explain God's far-reaching, inclusive love.

7. *Help your child feel good about himself or herself.* We are more likely to hate others if we hate ourselves. At the same time, don't defend another group by making this child feel bad about his or her own group. Equality is the goal. We are all equal in value because we are people created by God.

8. Not every type of prejudice is discussed in this short volume. Feel free to discuss any type of prejudice you may encounter.

You haven't chosen an easy task; but fortunately you have chosen the best time: while children are still young. May God make you wise and loving. May God help you show a child that there is a better way.

◆ ◆ ◆ ◆ ◆

We Are All Different

None of us is exactly like anyone else. Even identical twins aren't exactly the same. It may be their voices or their fingerprints or their hair, but somehow all people have "markings" that set them apart from anyone else.

God made many varieties of people. Each of us has something that is fascinatingly different from everyone else. If we get to know people from many races, nationalities, religions and experiences, we will find them more interesting than a dozen television shows.

If we reach out to meet people from all kinds of backgrounds, we will learn more about them and fear them less. We can celebrate the variety that God planned for our world. We can rejoice that God loves us all.

Bill Coleman

◆ ◆ ◆ ◆ ◆

Look, but Don't Stare

Suppose someone comes into a room and he looks different than most other people in the room. Should you look at him or turn your head away? Suppose the person is extremely tall or very overweight? What if he is in a wheelchair or on crutches?

His appearance has caught your attention; there is no denying that. Should you continue to look or should you turn your face to the wall?

Try this simple guideline. It works in almost every situation:

Look, but don't stare.
See, but don't gawk.

When someone whose appearance is different than yours enters a restaurant, it catches your eye. There is no sense in denying that. If the person is extremely attractive or obviously handicapped or in any way out of the ordinary, you are likely to notice him. (A person wearing a cat on his head would also get your attention!)

You notice because the person is different from you. If you saw the same person every day, you would barely notice the differences. A person carrying a live lizard will get your attention the first few days. After that, it starts to seem normal.

Sometimes children and adults act very immaturely when they see someone different. They point at the person or make fun of her or start giggling. It's terribly rude to act foolish over someone else's appearance.

Be sensitive about other people's feelings. It hurts when someone points at you or jokes about you too. We all need to consider how we make others feel.

All of us want to be treated politely and with dignity. We are people created by the same God. It would be cruel to make fun of someone because she has skin problems, poor body control, or can't walk.

We need to give everyone the same consideration.

Look, but don't stare.

See, but don't gawk.

How Many Kinds?

What do we think of when we think of prejudice? We hear so much about racial prejudice that we might think race is what it is all about. Actually there are many kinds of prejudice. Let's look at just a few to get us thinking.

Handicap prejudice. Not wanting people around if they are in wheelchairs or on crutches or are blind or have some other physical disability.

National or regional prejudice. Not liking someone just because he is from a certain place.

Money prejudice. Not liking people because they are either very rich or very poor.

Racial prejudice. Not wanting to be around people of a race that is different than yours.

Gender prejudice. A dislike for people of the opposite sex.

Old age prejudice. Disliking elderly people.

Child prejudice. A dislike for children.

Teen prejudice. Thinking all teenagers are rotten.

Religious prejudice. A distrust of religious people or a dislike of those from religions different than yours.

Appearance prejudice. A dislike for people you think don't look as good as you, or who you think look better than you.

Smarts prejudice. Ill feelings toward those you think are either smarter than you or not as smart as you.

Political prejudice. Disliking someone who has different political opinions than you do.

Social prejudice. Insiders reject outsiders, such as when a lawyer's child is not allowed to play with a janitor's child.

This list includes thirteen types of prejudice. Certainly we haven't thought of everything. Prejudice is more complicated and more widespread than you might think at first.

◆ ◆ ◆ ◆ ◆

In God's Image

All people, no matter what their skin color or nationality, have been created in the image of God. That means that in some ways we are like God. That means all of us can act in loving and caring ways. We don't always, but we can.

Since people are made in God's image, they deserve to be treated with respect. People are special. They are important both to God and to other people.

People of every religion, people of every gender, people with every sort of physical ability, people of every nation, people of every race—are created in the image of God.

There is no category of people that is better than any other kind of people. People should not be mistreated, ignored, ridiculed, hurt, or cheated. God doesn't want us to abuse each other in any way. When we look at others, we should remember that they are specially created by God.

"Then God said, 'Let us make man in our image, in our likeness'" (Genesis 1:26).

◆ ◆ ◆ ◆ ◆

Rich and Poor

Which one of these statements is true?

Rich people are selfish, greedy, and cruel.
Poor people are lazy, wasteful losers.

Actually neither statement is true. Some rich people are lazy, wasteful losers, just as some poor people are selfish, greedy, and cruel.

How people behave has little to do with how much money they have. It isn't fair to put labels on people. We each are free to behave however we like and our finances have little to do with it.

Making a broad statement about people is called stereotyping. If we say farmers grow corn, the statement is not entirely true. Some farmers grow corn, but not all farmers grow corn. Stereotyping says all farmers grow corn.

To say rich people are selfish, greedy, and cruel is a stereotype. The truth is that many rich people are kind, caring, and generous.

To say that a person is poor because she is lazy is wrong. When you meet a poor person, you may not know why he or she is poor. Some people are poor because they have too many medical bills to pay. Some people are poor because they have not had a good education. People are poor for many reasons. The people who are poor may be extremely creative and fun to be with.

Many good people are rich. Many good people are poor. The only way to know for sure is to get to know them as individuals.

Don't believe the stereotypes you hear. Every person is different.

◆ ◆ ◆ ◆ ◆

What Is Prejudice?

Prejudice. The word gets used a great deal. Someone is arrested by the police and complains that the police are prejudiced. A student is not selected for the basketball team and might say the coach is prejudiced. Maybe these accusations are true and maybe they aren't.

Prejudice means to prejudge. It means that you make up your mind about someone before you even get to know them. If you see a person wearing a black leather jacket and assume he is a bad character, you have prejudged that person. You have never met this person. You probably don't know his name. But you have already decided that he is trouble.

The fact is, he might be trouble. But this person also could be a cool, caring, friendly person who just happens to enjoy black leather jackets.

In this case you didn't know what the jacket meant, if it meant anything. You didn't have enough facts to make a decision. If you dislike a person simply because of his clothing or appearance, you have prejudice. You are judging someone without knowing all the facts.

Probably all of us are prejudiced. There are certain "kinds" of people we don't like. Maybe you don't like short people or rich people or fat people or white people or people who chew gum.

You might not like poor people or smart people or people in wheelchairs and you might not like adults. You may have a reason to dislike them, and you may *not* have a reason, but you dislike them anyway.

If you dislike a person you don't know, you show your prejudice. If you dislike an entire group of people (like Native Americans or football players or teachers), you show your prejudice.

Let's say it this way: if you dislike a person or group you do not know, you are prejudiced. You have judged them without getting to know them.

Is it different if the tall boy down the street picks on you and you dislike him? Yes! You have a reason to be upset at *that* tall boy. But if you then dislike *all* tall boys because of that one tall boy, you are being prejudiced.

To dislike people we have not met is unfair. But most of us do it sometime. We may even do it often. In order to stop doing it, we first have to understand what we are doing.

◆ ◆ ◆ ◆ ◆

They Called Jesus Names

Have you ever been called an ugly name—
the kind of name that makes your blood boil?
Maybe someone called you "stupid" or "goof
head." Maybe you have been called something
really nasty (the kind of name that we wouldn't
print in this book!).

Some names bounce off and we don't give
them much thought. Other names feel like a stab
in the heart.

It doesn't seem to matter who you are or
how nice you are, people still call you names.
When Jesus was on earth, he was called names.
If you were Jewish, as Jesus was, one of the worst
things anyone could call you was "Samaritan."
Samaritans were considered phoney Jews who
copied the Jewish religion. Most Jewish people
in Jesus' time would have nothing to do with
Samaritans.

One day some people were very angry at
Jesus. They didn't like what he said about the
love of God. Try to picture these people: angry,
red-faced, teeth clenched. Then one said, "Aren't
we right in saying that you are a Samaritan?"
(John 8:48).

The angry man knew Jesus wasn't a Samaritan. He simply felt nasty and this was the
ugliest thing he could think of to call him.

Jesus refused to treat Samaritans badly. He became their friend. He told them about the love of God. Jesus told a story and made one of them the hero (the story of the Good Samaritan, Luke 10:25-37.) The Son of God wasn't uptight about Samaritans.

Jesus knows what it's like to be called names, names that aren't fair. He knows what it's like to be disliked and even hated. People hated him so much they even murdered him.

It hurts to be called names. That's why many of us refuse to call people names. We don't like to be hurt and we choose not to hurt others.

♦ ♦ ◆ ♦ ♦

Why Do We Laugh?

Why do we laugh at people who are different? Have you ever made fun of a blind person with a long white cane? Have you ever laughed at someone who walked with twisted legs? Maybe you or your friends have giggled at someone who has crooked teeth.

Most of us have made fun of someone, but why do we do it? There are several reasons why we ridicule others. Let's look at a few.

1. *We are mischievous.* We might make fun of an old woman just to laugh. Children and adults make fun of others often and they do it without meaning any harm. Making fun is normal. It may not be wise, but it is normal.

   Every night comedians on television make fun of people and we all laugh. There is something daring and exciting about it.

   But poking fun at someone can be hurtful. If we stop to think of how our teasing might harm someone, we probably won't do it.

2. *We are afraid.* If we see something that frightens us, we sometimes try to joke about it. When we see a person with a

mental disability, we may not know how to react to that person. Uncomfortable with the situation, we laugh because we don't know what else to do.

Since we don't know what to say to a person in a wheelchair, it may be easier to make fun of her in front of our friends. Laughter breaks the tension. We don't know what to do so we clown around.

3. *Some people are unkind.* We hate to admit this, but it's true. Some people laugh at others because they want to hurt their feelings. This is no accident or release of nervous tension. They want to embarrass someone simply because she is different.

Burning a cross in someone's yard is wrong.

Stoning the house of an Asian couple is wrong.

Battering the car of a white family is wrong.

Writing on the walls of a synagogue is wrong.

Yelling threats at an Hispanic family is wrong.

It is one thing if we accidently hurt someone's feelings; it is quite another if we *try* to hurt that person. It's dangerous to laugh at people who are different than ourselves. But it is evil to try to hurt them. None of us should try to get fun out of making fun of others.

Homeless People

Millions of people in the world have no permanent or regular homes. They live in cars, in abandoned buildings, in alleys, on empty lots, and in cardboard shanties. Some homeless people are adults. Some are children. Some live with their families. Others, as young as nine years old, are entirely on their own.

Maybe you have seen pictures of homeless people. Maybe you have seen them on the news. Maybe you have seen homeless people on the streets of your town. You may have questions about people who have no homes: Who are they? How did they get there? What are they like? What will become of them?

Life on the streets is hard. It can be dangerous. It is not a happy existence. Few people would choose to live in a cardboard box.

It can be frightening to see people who live on the streets. Often we try to avoid them because they appear dirty, or sick, or drunk. Still, some churches, missions, and other organizations work hard to feed and clothe homeless people. The numbers are so great that these groups have trouble meeting all the needs. Their work is made more difficult because society tends to have contempt for homeless people rather than compassion.

Jesus loves each homeless person. Sometimes it is difficult for us to love people the same way Jesus does. Our fears and our prejudices get in the way. Jesus wants us to try. He also wants us to help them in whatever way we can.

"Then the righteous will answer him, 'Lord, when did we see you hungry and feed you, or thirsty and give you something to drink? When did we see you a stranger and invite you in, or needing clothes and clothe you? When did we see you sick or in prison and go to visit you?

"The King will reply, 'I tell you the truth, whatever you did for one of the least of these brothers of mine, you did for me' " (Matthew 25:37-40).

◆ ◆ ◆ ◆ ◆

Gifted Children

When Jerry's mother came home, she knew something was wrong. The normally energetic, playful fifth grader was sitting in the living room, slumped down in a chair.

"What's wrong, Jerry?" his mother asked hesitantly as she removed her coat.

"I didn't make it," he grumbled.

"You didn't make what?" she asked as she sat on the couch.

"That stupid gifted program. Sarah made it, but I didn't."

"That really hurt, didn't it?" His mother frowned.

"I'm just not gifted, I guess. I wanted to be gifted but I guess I'm not good enough."

"You may not have made the program," Jerry's mother continued, "but that doesn't mean you aren't gifted. Every person is gifted. We are simply gifted in different ways."

"The school said I'm not gifted," Jerry growled. "If I was gifted, they would have chosen me for the program."

"That really isn't it," his mother explained. "They were looking for people who are gifted in certain skills like English or math. There are a lot more gifts than those.

"For instance, you might have the gift of being a good friend. Or you may have the gift of being creative. What about the gift of being patient? Or working with your hands?"

"Those things don't make you gifted," Jerry objected.

"I disagree. I think those are the most important gifts of all. Being able to multiply 46 times 46 in your head is one kind of gift. But the gift of caring about others is a really special gift."

"Yeah, but you feel like a dork if you can't multiply in your head," Jerry complained.

"There are some folks who can't think well enough to pass in school but they are gifted, too," Mother insisted. "We are simply gifted in different ways."

"I sure don't feel gifted."

"Gifted doesn't mean you are better than someone else." Jerry's mother stood up. "It just means there is something you have to offer. Think about what you have to offer, Jerry."

"Each one should use whatever gift he has received to serve others" (1 Peter 4:10).

The Boy Who Could Not Walk

In ancient Israel there was a boy named Mephibosheth (pronounced Me-FIB-o-sheth). When he was five years old his grandfather Saul and his father Jonathan were killed. When Mephibosheth's nurse heard the terrible news, she hurried to hide the boy. Unfortunately in her haste she tripped and fell on his leg. The accident was so severe that Mephibosheth could never walk again.

Years later, King David wanted to do something kind for the fallen family of Jonathan. Asking how he might help, David soon learned about the son who couldn't walk. By now Mephibosheth had married and led a quiet life. David wanted to see Jonathan's son.

When Mephibosheth arrived to see the king, the young man was quite afraid. Usually conquering kings were not kind, and he worried about his fate.

Punishment was the farthest thing from King David's mind. Instead, he honored Mephibosheth and treated him with dignity.

First, he gave Mephibosheth back the estate that his grandfather once had. He also assigned someone to manage the land.

Second, David invited Mephibosheth to eat daily at the king's table. He accepted the young man as royalty, exactly as the king would treat others in this position.

Despite his disability, Mephibosheth was welcomed with all the privileges and friendship of anyone whom the king honored. The fact that he could not walk presented no obstacle to total acceptance by a caring king.

Mephibosheth was valuable as a person. The king refused to cast him out or hide him in the background. He would be treated well by a king who was not shaken by Mephibosheth's inability to walk.

"Accept one another, then, just as Christ accepted you" (Romans 15:7).

Friends Who Are Different

It isn't that Mona looks for friends who are different. She doesn't start each day searching for someone who came from a foreign country or someone who wears unusual clothes. But Mona is friends with people from many backgrounds, and she learns from each of them.

One of her favorites is a young boy from Germany. He brought over a picture album showing beautiful mountains that he had climbed with his parents. He likes to listen to music and play games on the computer. Mona learns from her German friend and they laugh over the silliest things.

She has another friend who lives in Apartment 345. Her name is Tina. Tina likes singing and photography. Mona and Tina are very much alike. The only difference is that Tina uses a wheelchair. Mona has learned that people in wheelchairs aren't much different than people out of wheelchairs, except that they can't walk.

Mona has a special friend named Stephanie. The biggest difference between them is that they don't have the same skin color. Stephanie's skin is light, almost pink, while Mona's skin is dark, not quite tan and yet not quite brown either. Mona learns from Stephanie. Her friend doesn't seem to notice their difference in skin color. If she does, she doesn't mention it. Mona found out that color or race don't seem to matter with some people.

Another friend is a girl named Lea. If Mona stopped to think about it, Lea is quite a bit over-weight. But, to tell the truth, Mona never stops to think about it. They don't have time to com-pare weight with each other or discuss diets. They have places to go and things to do. Once a week they play volleyball after school. And they go to painting classes. Mona is working on a portrait of a gorgeous brown horse and Lea is painting a windmill. They don't have time to stare at each other's waistlines. Weight doesn't make much difference to two happy friends.

It might be fun to have a friend who looks, talks, acts, and thinks exactly like you. But it could be even more exciting to have friends who are "unlike" us. Friends who are different can open our minds to new experiences we might otherwise miss.

◆ ◆ ◆ ◆ ◆

Other Religions

"Why do you go to church on Saturday?" Shane asked his friend Alex.

"It's just what we believe, I guess." Alex reloaded the VCR. "Our family has always gone on Saturday mornings."

"Well, it sounds so goofy," Shane blurted out. "No offense, I mean. But most people go to church on Sunday, don't they?"

"I don't know," Alex admitted. "Most of the people I know go on Saturday."

"But I mean, do you worship God and all that stuff?" Shane asked.

"You must think we practice voodoo or stick needles in cats or something weird like that," Alex said.

"It isn't that," Shane protested. "You seem all right, and your parents are nice people and all."

"So, even though we don't practice religion the same way or on the same day, we can still be nice people. Doesn't that make sense?" Alex asked.

"Must be true, Shane said. "You don't seem weird to me. Let's get this movie started."

Alex's religion was different than Shane's, but that didn't make Alex or his family bad.

Shane didn't agree with the way Alex practiced his religion but that didn't make Alex less important than Shane.

If we believe in Jesus Christ as our Savior, we should be happy about our faith. But our faith doesn't make us better than anyone else. Because we are Christians we can love those who don't agree with us about our religion.

Sometimes Christians forget and make fun of other people's religious beliefs and practices. We start to joke about their holidays or their practices or their food. We might even kid about the clothes their ministers wear or the language they use. It's easy to become mean and cruel in the way we talk about others.

If we don't agree with another religion, we should at least show respect. Christians shouldn't be rude or insulting about the practices of other groups.

When we love the Christian faith, we don't have to hate someone else's church or synagogue or temple or meeting place. We can love ours and show respect for theirs.

◆ ◆ ◆ ◆ ◆

Changing Your Mind

We change all the time.

We change socks.
We change channels.
We change hairstyles.

Sometimes change is hard, but we manage to do it. Change may be difficult; but when we are determined, change can happen.

We change tapes.
We change videos.
We change breakfast cereals.

Wouldn't life be dull if you never changed? Imagine if you still played with the puzzles you had in preschool.

We change clothes.
We change bedtimes.
We change our rooms around.

Suppose you never changed shoes. As you grew, your foot size would get larger, but somehow you would keep on wearing the same shoes.

We change attitudes.
We change habits.
We even change friends.

All of us can change. We do it all the time.
We can also change how we feel about others.

How we feel about elderly people.
How we feel about noisy people.
How we feel about teachers.
How we feel about neighbors.

If you aren't comfortable about how you
feel, remember, it is all right to change your mind.

♦ ♦ ◆ ♦ ♦

Peter's Problem

When the church first began, the apostle Peter was eager to tell the good news about Jesus Christ. He loved to preach and teach. Because of his work, thousands of people were baptized and gave their lives to the Son of God.

One day, three men came to visit Peter. They had been sent by a man named Cornelius who was a Roman military officer, a Gentile. Gentile means he was not Jewish, as Peter was.

Peter had been taught that as a Jewish person, he should have nothing to do with Gentiles. It was hard for him to believe that God would want him to go to the house of Cornelius. But God had given Peter a vision that showed him it was all right to associate with Gentiles. And so Peter went with the three men.

When Peter arrived at Cornelius's house, it was packed with people. Cornelius told Peter that he had been praying for someone to come and teach him and his family about the commandments of God. Peter explained that even though the Jewish laws said he should not associate with Gentiles, God seemed to be telling him it would be okay. Peter then taught the people who had assembled, and more people gave their lives to Jesus that day.

If Peter had not heeded God's gracious word that Gentiles were welcome to come to God too, those people at Cornelius's house might never have heard the good news. When we shut out people who are different from us, we miss the chance of spreading the good news, too. Let's take a cue from Peter.

"Then Peter began to speak; 'I now realize how true it is that God does not show favoritism but accepts men from every nation who fear him and do what is right' " (Acts 10:34-35).

◆ ◆ ◆ ◆ ◆

God's Favorite

Most of us have a favorite color. You might even have two or three favorites. I like to wear my tan jacket or my blue one. This past year my favorite sweater has been cream colored. I wear if often, even sometimes when it should be put in the laundry!

When it comes to color, we like one better than another. That's understandable when we are talking about clothes or cars or towels.

But when we talk about skin color, it shouldn't make any difference. Whether we have pink skin or tan or dark or light doesn't matter. In fact, the color of a person's skin is the least important thing about a person.

God's people come in all colors and shades and tones. They have all kinds of hair and all sizes of ears and noses and feet. There is no good skin or bad skin. No good races or bad races.

Do you ever wonder what kind of people God likes best? Is there a certain favored race or nationality? Does God like farmers more than airline pilots? Does God like boys better than girls? Does God like ministers better than football players?

The Bible answers that question for us. God sent his Son, Jesus, to earth because God loves all of us equally. God doesn't have favorites.

God loves boys, girls, cooks, doctors, construction workers, and jugglers all just the same. God also loves rich people, poor people, swimmers, and homemakers exactly alike.

Jesus Christ died on the cross and later rose from the dead because he cared about every person, everywhere.

God loves people who go to church and people who don't go to church. God loves people who live in mansions as well as those who live on the street. God loves people with AIDS and those who never get a cold. God loves overweight people and skinny people and those who ride to work on skates.

God doesn't have any favorites because God loves us all.

"There is neither Jew nor Greek, slave nor free, male nor female, for you are all one in Christ Jesus" (Galatians 3:28).

◆ ◆ ◆ ◆ ◆

Ignorance Hurts

Which of these sayings have you heard?

- Parents who are divorced must not love their children very much, otherwise they would have stayed together.
- It would be better to put children who have disabilities in institutions.
- God gives people AIDS to punish them.
- Adults who never marry are gay or lesbian.
- Children in other countries aren't loved as much by parents as children in this country.
- White people and African-Americans can't get along.
- Rich people are smarter than poor people.

These are called generalities. Maybe you have heard some of them. Maybe you haven't heard any. Generalities are prejudices because they tend to put an entire group of people into one statement.

Usually prejudice is based on ignorance. We don't know the facts so we push everybody under one statement. If we are to erase our prejudices, we have to learn more.

Let's take time to learn the truth about each of these statements.

- Many divorced parents not only love their children but work hard to help them.
- Some children with disabilities need to be in institutions for their own care. But most get along very well living in their own homes.
- Many people have AIDS through no fault of their own. Never assume that God has punished someone with a disease.
- Some single adults are gay or lesbian—most are not.
- There are parents everywhere who don't love their children. However, many parents in all countries love their children with all their hearts.
- In many work and school situations, white and African-Americans get along extremely well, but people in both groups still suffer from not knowing each other better.
- Some of the smartest people have jobs that pay only small salaries.

Many false statements are passed around. To reduce prejudice, we need to learn more.

Jesus told us that if we knew the truth we could be set free from the power of sin. If we know the truth about people we can also be set free from prejudice.

"Then you will know the truth, and the truth will set you free" (John 8:32).

◆ ◆ ◆ ◆ ◆

From Totoland

A new family moved into Mindy's neighborhood. The family came from another country. Let's make up a name for that country and call it Totoland.

Mindy had never actually met anyone from Totoland, but she had heard plenty. Her Uncle Ben told her stories about people from there. He called them Totos.

Her uncle said the Totos couldn't be trusted. He said they were sneaky. According to him they would lie and steal and Mindy would be smart to hide her bicycle.

Besides, said Uncle Ben, he was sure they ate weird foods that smelled funny. Not only that, he continued, but their religion was very strange. He'd been told that they burned herbs and spices when they prayed.

Uncle Ben's description of the Toto family gave Mindy the chills. She didn't want to get close to anyone who did all those horrible things. Mindy became afraid of her new neighbors and tried hard to stay away from them.

Fear is a terrible feeling. It's hard to get to know people if we are afraid of them. If Mindy had gotten to know the Toto family she might have found them to be great friends. She might have enjoyed their tasty foods and liked their music. She might have learned neat things about their country.

Many false stories are spread around that can make us feel afraid.

When you hear terrible stories about the people from Totoland—or from anywhere else—you should go directly to your parents or another trusted adult. They are good at figuring out the truth and telling children what they need to know.

If we are afraid of people, we can't love them. We're too afraid to even get close. Much of the time we are afraid when we don't need to be.

We should be afraid of some people. They could hurt us. But most people are gentle and kind. Wise adults can help us discover which people are which.

◆ ◆ ◆ ◆ ◆

Sticks and Stones

Katie was one of the shortest kids in the fifth grade. She wasn't sure if she would be short all of her life. All Katie knew was that so far she wasn't as big as she liked, and it bothered her.

Her height was a problem in two of her classes. During gym class she was usually chosen last for basketball. She could dribble but she wasn't tall enough to shoot well.

In English class Toby liked to call her "Shorty," and the name was starting to spread. Katie liked her real name and hated to be called that miserable nickname.

Katie's Aunt Sarah lived two blocks away. One day while baking cookies with her aunt, she explained what bugged her about the nickname.

Aunt Sarah was pretty cool and didn't rattle easily. As she cut cookies with an upside down jar, Aunt Sarah told Katie that size didn't mean much. Character, kindness, honesty, and thoughtfulness are far more important than height or weight.

Aunt Sarah also told her a rhyme she had learned as a girl. It went like this: "Sticks and stones may break my bones, but words will never hurt me."

When people had called her names, she would repeat this little rhyme and it made her feel better. She knew that words will only hurt if we let them.

From that day on Katie stored Aunt Sarah's rhyme in the back of her brain. When someone called her a name, Katie would whisper it to herself. Even when Katie became an adult and worked in an office, she remembered that rhyme.

When someone made a dumb remark about the dress she wore, Katie just smiled at the person and thought to herself, "Sticks and stones may break my bones, but words will never hurt me."

"The Lord does not look at the things man looks at. Man looks at the outward appearance, but the Lord looks at the heart" (1 Samuel 16:7).

◆ ◆ ◆ ◆ ◆

Let's Be Silly

Suppose you see a man coming down the street toward you and he looks very angry. He is carrying a gun in one hand and a hammer in the other. A hunting knife is wedged firmly in his teeth.

Should you say, "I don't want to judge this person. After all I barely know him. Maybe he is just a local gardener and he is on his way to kill weeds on a lawn. Maybe I should introduce myself. I don't want to appear prejudiced. I think I'll invite him over and make popcorn."

That's dumb. You have plenty of facts about this person. Run! Hide! Call the police! This man looks dangerous.

Yes, it's a silly illustration. But it makes a point. Don't try to get to know everybody. Steer clear of anyone who might hurt you. Tell your parents or other trusted adult if someone tries to hurt you.

That isn't dealing with prejudice; that's dealing with reality.

♦ ♦ ♦ ♦ ♦

Mentally Challenged

All of us have limits to our mental abilities. Even the smartest person in the world can't think of everything all the time. And some people who are extremely bright in one subject may not do so well in another. Some people might be able to read very well, but they might have trouble multiplying numbers.

Some people learn quickly from what they hear.

Some people learn quickly from what they see.

Some people learn better from what they can feel or do.

What about you? How do you learn best?

We shouldn't expect everyone to have the same mental ability. Some people could be called "mechanical geniuses." They know exactly what to do to fix an engine. But those same people may not have read a book in years. These people aren't stupid. Their interests and abilities just run in a certain direction.

Some people have mental abilities that are far below what is considered average. Their ability to think is limited to the point that they appear different from others. These people are said to have a mental disability. Another way to describe their abilities is to say they are mentally challenged.

Mentally challenged people are often made fun of. They are called mean names like "Retard" and "Moron" or "Dummy." Sometimes people think these names are funny, but they aren't.

Mentally challenged people have gifts to contribute. They offer love, kindness, sharing, and thoughtfulness to those around them. Mentally challenged people deserve respect.

Just because a person has difficulty learning in traditional ways doesn't mean that person is not able to learn. Just because someone may have a mental disability, doesn't mean that person can't be good at sports or music or making friends.

People who are mentally challenged are real people. They may be limited in some ways, but we all are limited to some degree. Mentally challenged people are also gifted because they have abilities that others may not share. If people act differently than others or talk differently or eat differently, their differences do not make them bad. Different isn't bad. It's just different!

When the Bible says that God so loved the world, it means God loved everyone. God didn't send his Son just because he loved star athletes and winners of spelling contests. God loves us all, regardless of our learning abilities.

"God so loved the world that he gave his one and only Son, that *whoever* believes in him shall not perish but have eternal life" (John 3:16, emphasis added).

◆ ◆ ◆ ◆ ◆

Learn a Better Way

When you were born, there were some things you did naturally. You could drink and cry and mess your diapers without being told to. The hospital didn't offer a class for babies on how to throw up. Your body knew how to do these things when you left your mother's womb.

Other things were harder. As you grew older adults had to teach you to stop throwing food. They taught you how to hold a spoon. Before long they helped you learn to say words.

Some things are natural and some things are taught.

Is prejudice natural or something we learn? Were we born afraid of people who are different from us, or did we learn it later?

We weren't born believing boys or girls are better. We didn't roll over in the hospital nursery, look at the baby next to us and say, "Yuck, it's a boy." We had to learn that prejudice.

That's good news. God didn't create us already prejudiced. We didn't lie in the doctor's arms and cry, "I hate tall people." Prejudice is something we learned later.

How did we learn to dislike certain kinds of people? There are many ways it could happen.

Parents may have taught us.

Teachers may have taught us.

Brothers, sisters, or other relatives may have taught us.

Some churches may have taught us.

We may have had a bad experience with someone and we assumed that everyone like that was bad.

We learn prejudice in many different ways.

Why is that good news? Since we had to learn prejudice, we can also unlearn it. We don't have to be hopelessly prejudiced. We can learn to respect and like all kinds of people.

We weren't born prejudiced. We can learn the truth and find out that good people come in all shapes and sizes.

◆ ◆ ◆ ◆ ◆

Discrimination

Discrimination. The word simply means to pick and choose. All of us need to be discriminating. For example, if you cook food that is old or spoiled, you can get sick from eating it. So you choose fresh food. Smart people are discriminating because they pick and choose.

You need to be discriminating. For example, if you wear socks with poor elastic at the top, your socks will keep falling down around your ankles. Try to select socks that will stay up when you want them to stay up.

When you pick friends, discrimination is very important. Never choose a friend who likes to get in trouble, someone who steals, sneaks into places, fools with drugs, or is a terrible friend. Eventually he or she will get caught and you could be in trouble too.

Discrimination is a good word. Every smart person is discriminating about something.

But sometimes we discriminate about the wrong things. If we pick and choose friends on the basis of:

race,
nationality,
physical ability,
gender (male or female),

money,
religion,
~~or something like that,~~

we discriminate for the wrong reasons.

Choose your friends carefully. Be discriminating. But be sure to discriminate for the right reasons.

◆ ◆ ◆ ◆ ◆

A Proud Heritage

When my family first moved to midwestern America, we looked for Indians. We expected to see them as we had in old movies, with painted faces and war bonnets atop galloping horses. We were surprised to discover that much of what our family believed about Indians, or Native Americans, just wasn't true.

Native Americans are more than what the movies projected. They are a proud nation made up of many tribes, and their culture is rich in traditions that can be traced back many centuries. For example, they have always revered the earth and all that is in it. Native Americans are also a people who have been treated badly in the past. They were forced from the vast lands they called home onto poor reservation land. They were denied the legal rights that white people enjoyed.

Today, Native Americans have legal rights the same as everyone. They do not have to live on reservations, though many still do. Native Americans can be found in almost every walk of American life. But that does not mean that all prejudice against Native Americans has vanished. Too many people still believe that the old movies were true.

A similar story could be told about Hispanic people, African-Americans, people from Southeast Asia, Arabs, and others whose heritage is not Northern European. Like Native Americans, they too have suffered discrimination. It doesn't make sense when you stop to think about it. But not everyone stops to think.

The world is made up of a wide diversity of people. God created all of them, each with unique talents and gifts. We can celebrate the rich variety of traditions and foods and music and culture that the world has to offer. As God's children, we don't have to settle for what the movies tell us!

Simeon, the Niger

The Bible doesn't spend much time discussing races or the color of a person's skin. There are a few references, but not many. That's probably because to God, all people are the same.

A couple of Christ's early disciples suggest that some of the early believers were Africans.

God sent Philip on the road to Gaza where he met an Ethiopian who worked for the queen named Candace. The Ethiopian was reading the Bible. After a short conversation, he asked Philip if he could be baptized. Philip was happy to baptize this new believer in Jesus Christ. (See Acts 8:26-40.)

Another interesting person is found in the church at Antioch. Listed among the prophets and teachers is a man named Simeon, the Niger. *Niger* is the Latin word for black.

Why was Simeon called "the black"? Did he like to wear black robes and black sandals? Was his hair jet black? Or was he called the Niger because his skin was black? (See Acts 13:1.)

We may never know the real answer to Simeon's identity. However, there is good reason to believe that the disciples were integrated by race from the very beginning.

Jesus never excluded anyone on the basis of race or nationality. He welcomed everyone who wanted to be a part of the family of God.

"I no longer call you servants . . . Instead I have called you friends" (John 15:15).

Who Is Better: Boys or Girls?

Put two boys and two girls in a room. Give each a piece of paper and a pencil. Then put this math problem on the board:

$$2789 \\ + \ 3842$$

Tell them to start. Who will get the correct answer in the shortest amount of time? Will the girls add faster or the boys?

Next, ask the same two boys and two girls to guess time. When you say "go," each person should say when he or she thinks one minute has passed. You have the only watch. Write down how close each person comes to the one-minute mark.

Will boys or girls do better at this test?

Let's try one more. Take one pound of cheese and a one-pound onion. Hold one in your right hand and one in your left. If you drop them both at the same time, which one will hit the floor first?

Will the girls get the correct answer first or will the boys win?

The answer to all three questions is exactly the same. Whether the boys or the girls get the correct answers first depends on who the boys and girls are.

It would be wrong to say: Megan does math better than David because Megan is a girl. That's prejudice.

Do girls cook better than boys? That depends on who the girl is and who the boy is.

Can boys climb better than girls? Which boy and which girl are you talking about?

Who are the best skaters? You can't tell until they learn to skate.

Many of us grew up with gender prejudices. (Gender means male or female.) We believed that girls are good at some things while boys are good at other things.

But some girls can out-wrestle some boys. Some boys can sew better than some girls. It all depends on who the boy and girl happen to be.

Today, it is more common for girls and boys to have equal opportunities, to try things they want to. But old prejudices still exist. We have to work hard to break down the walls. Boys aren't better than girls and girls aren't better than boys.

◆ ◆ ◆ ◆ ◆

What Color Is God?

When you close your eyes and try to picture God, what color do you see? Is God dark complexioned or pink? Do you imagine God as an Asian or a Native American or an Arab, or what?

Since none of us has seen God, we can't say exactly what God's color is. God is a Spirit. God doesn't have skin in the same way we have.

The Bible tells us, "God is spirit, and his worshipers must worship in spirit and in truth" (John 4:24).

How can you picture God in your mind if God doesn't have skin? The most important part of us is our character. Character means how we treat others. We know that God loves all people. So when you think about God, think about what God does, not about God's skin color.

No Answers

Everyone broke into laughter as Luke sat down, embarrassed. He couldn't remember the capital of New York state. Whenever he thought he had a chance, Luke would raise his hand and volunteer to answer. But sometimes when he was on his feet, Luke had trouble thinking. Too often he wouldn't say anything and then he would blush and sit down.

A few of the other kids would tease Luke about his problem. They called him names and would pull tricks on him. Soon Luke became shy and didn't like to try anymore.

It's hard to say what will happen in Luke's life. Maybe he will learn better as he grows older. He might learn to be good at some subjects and not at others. It's possible that Luke will never do well at classroom subjects.

Whatever Luke does in the classroom, hopefully he will meet some friends who will help him gain confidence. He may get better at speaking. They will accept and enjoy being around him just because Luke is a nice person. Those people won't make fun of Luke because they will learn what he is really like.

If someone knows all about reading but picks on others who can't read as well, that person is missing something.

If someone gets great grades but makes fun of slow learners, that person doesn't know enough about love.

If someone thinks she is better than others because she can remember history dates, she is too proud.

The ability to learn and to learn well is important. But it isn't the only part of life. To love God, to be kind, to be forgiving, to help others: these are far more important than learning fast and getting good grades.

Some people will get to know Luke. They won't care whether he can speak in public or not. They will find out that he is a good friend, fun to be around, and someone who won't do you dirty.

Neither slow learning nor fast learning ever made someone a good person.

We Come in All Sizes

Make yourself a pledge. Try to keep it all of your life. It goes like this: I will not make anyone's life miserable by making fun of his or her body.

The size of a person's body has nothing to do with his or her character. Good friends come in all kinds of packages. Good friends come in small bodies, in twisted bodies, in average bodies, in large bodies.

Don't make people feel bad about themselves by calling their body names. Some feel bad all their lives because of the terrible things that people have said.

Remember the pledge: I will not make anyone's life miserable by making fun of his or her body.

◆ ◆ ◆ ◆ ◆

Special Clothes

Some people dress according to religious rules. They wear special hats or suits or dresses because of their beliefs. Others shave their heads or grow beards or refuse to wear makeup as part of their dedication to God.

If we make fun of people who dress differently than we do, we show our own immaturity. Mature people learn to respect the religious clothing or appearance of others.

Some Jewish men wear a skullcap called a yarmulke. Often they wear them only at home or in the synagogue. However, you might see them at other places also.

Many Amish men wear plain black suits with black hats. They also might have beards. But not all Amish men dress alike. Some prefer the simple way of life and do not own cars. Others have no electricity in their homes. They believe it is easier to live a godly life if they keep things plain.

Nuns often wear dark dresses called habits. This usually includes a head covering. Some nuns wear them whenever they are in public but other nuns seldom wear habits.

Often monks will shave their heads as part of their devotion to God. Buddhist monks look for ways to purify themselves.

Many Protestant and Catholic ministers wear special collars. This allows them to be immedlately identified as clergy in churches and hospitals.

Usually we make fun of people we don't understand. We don't have to agree with people in order to respect them. If you don't wear sandals or shave your head, you can still be kind to those who do.

You may not agree with the people who sing chants or collect money at airports, but that doesn't mean you have a right to laugh at them. It's their choice. As long as we don't bother each other, we should be allowed to dress as we like, or dress as we believe God wants us to dress.

By being kind to and tolerant of people who dress differently from us, we put on the garments of love.

◆ ◆ ◆ ◆ ◆

Red Hats and Green Pants

Long ago, around the turn of the century, there was a war. The people with the red hats fought the people who wore green pants. It was a terrible war which lasted for more than three years. Many people were killed and injured on both sides.

When the war ended, the people who wore red hats returned to their villages. They buried their dead and nursed their injured back to health. The people of the green pants did the same thing.

Soon they went back to their jobs working on farms and making shoes and running banks. Each village minded its own business. Their children went to school, families went to church and they went sleigh riding in the winter.

Though the two villages never fought again, neither did they forget each other. Late in the evening when families sat around the fire, father or mother would tell their children about the terrible war at the turn of the century. Parents would remind their children that they should hate the people of the other village. And when their children had children, the same stories were told all over again.

This happened in both villages.

Almost a hundred years later the same stories were being told to children. And the children of red hat villages hated the children of green pants villages, even though they had never met. And the children of the green pants villages hated the red hat children.

When these children grow up and have children of their own, will they sit around the fire and tell the same stories? Will they teach their children to hate the people of the other village? Or will they finally forgive the people who fought the war almost a hundred years ago? How can they stop the stories?

♦ ♦ ◆ ♦ ♦

Which of These Are True?

Take this quick quiz and answer true or false.

1. Smart kids are nerds.
2. African-American kids are on welfare.
3. White kids are prejudiced.
4. Jews are wealthy.
5. Rich people are dishonest.
6. Hispanics won't work.
7. Street people are lazy.
8. Long-haired men use drugs.
9. Poor people are dumb.
10. Athletes are stuck-up.
11. Women are whiners.
12. Brothers are brats.
13. Parents don't understand.

How well did you do on the quiz? The answer to all 13 is false. But then again the answer to all 13 is true.

If you want to know the truth, this quiz isn't fair. For instance: Some rich people are dishonest. But some rich people are also honest. It all depends on the rich person.

Some white kids are prejudiced. But some white kids try hard to be fair, accepting, and understanding. It all depends on who the white kid is.

People aren't as simple as this quiz makes them look. We are all complicated. Some Jewish people have lots of money, others have average incomes, and some are definitely poor. It all depends on which Jewish person you are talking about.

Athletes can be stuck-up and arrogant. They can also be caring, kind, and considerate. It all depends on the athlete.

The only way to pass the quiz is to answer each question true and false. Some long-haired men do use drugs but most of them don't.

This may be hard to believe. Some of us have believed since we were born that certain types of people act certain ways. If we hear that an African-American family lives on welfare, we might believe that every African-American family needs welfare. Like every kind of people, some families need welfare and some families don't.

The more we learn about other races and nationalities and people who are different than we are, the better we can accept each other. Hate and fear usually come from ignorance.

Take the quiz again. This time remember that the answer to each question is true and false.

◆ ◆ ◆ ◆ ◆

You Talk Funny

Everybody speaks with an accent. When people from another nation or another part of the country or another race hear us talk, they think we have an accent. Some people in California and some people in Massachusetts say the words "car" and "Cuba" and "idea" with a different accent.

Someone in Montana and someone in Mississippi may say the word "oil" differently. People on the Eastern Shore of Maryland and people in Chicago will probably say "boat" with different accents.

Sometimes people living in the same country, speaking the same language have trouble understanding each other. An accent means we say the same word but we give it a slightly different sound.

How do people say "either" where you live? Do they pronounce it "eether" or "eyether"? Do you say "neither" as "neether" or "nyther"? It depends on your accent. Sometimes people living on the same block or in the same apartment building pronounce words very differently.

There isn't anything wrong with having an accent. All of us have some kind of accent. The problem comes when we start to think that people who speak differently are somehow inferior to us. We are tempted to laugh at someone with a midwestern accent or an Hispanic accent or a Boston accent. We think that people with accents must be stupid.

Of course, there is no truth to this at all. If we stop and think about it, we know that someone who speaks differently is not inferior to us or to anyone else. They don't pronounce words the same, but inside we are exactly the same kind of human beings.

Many of the people who knew Jesus and his disciples could hear their accents. Jesus grew up in an area called Galilee. When he visited Jerusalem in the area of Judea, his listeners could tell that he pronounced his words differently.

Some people wouldn't trust a person with a Galilean accent. They thought that God couldn't be with someone from that area of the country.

It's too bad that they missed this special gift from God. They simply refused to accept Jesus as the Son of God because they wouldn't stop to hear someone with an accent.

When we are turned off by someone with an accent, remember that we have accents, too. So did Jesus and his disciples.

"After a little while, those standing there went up to Peter and said, 'Surely you are one of them, for your accent gives you away'" (Matthew 26:73).

The Blind Missionary

Lenny was born without sight. As he grew up, Lenny learned to adapt to a world he could not see. Eager to participate, he tried sports, sciences, and education. He jumped into any activity that his seeing friends would let him try. Sometimes Lenny pushed himself into situations even when others tried to stop him.

The energetic kid got his share of bumps and bruises like everyone else. When he became a teenager, Lenny went out for wrestling and became a champion. At the same time he prepared himself for college. He was determined to get everything out of life that he could.

While in college, Lenny felt strongly that God had called him to be a missionary. He wanted to go to another country and tell people about the love of Jesus Christ. Everyone seemed surprised that Lenny would want to try anything so difficult. But Lenny didn't like having doors closed on him so he picked his classes carefully and prepared himself.

When Lenny thought the time was right, he applied to a missionary board and told them about his plans. They listened carefully. The board members were amazed that this young man who was blind could imagine himself in a foreign country. The language would be a problem, transportation would be difficult, proper housing would be hard to find. The board rejected him.

All of his life Lenny had learned to rise above discouragement. He applied to a second mission board. They saw sincerity and sense of commitment. After weighing their decision thoroughly, the board accepted this man of commitment and sent him to the mission field.

Lenny spent most of his adult life in another country telling others about the love of Christ. Others had seen his blindness as an obstacle that he would not be able to overcome. Lenny saw it as a problem he could rise above and conquer.

Our first impulse is often to protect people with disabilities. We don't want them to get hurt or to hurt anyone else. Often all they want is the opportunity to try.

◆ ◆ ◆ ◆ ◆

Which Is More Important?

If you were picking friends, which would you choose?
   a. Someone who could read rapidly but was insulting and rude? or
   b. Someone who could read slowly but was kind and considerate?
Pick one. Is ability more important than love?

Would you select?
   a. Someone who can sing but who steals your belongings? or
   b. Someone who can't carry a tune but always returns what he or she borrows?
Pick one.

Would you rather know:
   a. Someone who is a good basketball player but never shares the ball? or
   b. Someone who is an average basketball player but lets the other players shoot too?
Pick one.

Who would you like to spend time with?
   a. Someone who calls you names and bosses you around? or
   b. Someone who speaks kindly to you and shares?
Pick one.

WHICH IS MORE IMPORTANT?

Too often we accept the fastest, tallest, most intelligent, strongest people as the most important. But all people are important. In a foot race, the person who comes in twenty-fifth is just as important as the one who finishes first. They don't have equal ability, but they are equally important. They are important because they are people, not because they are fast.

A man in my town appears to have the mental ability of a child. When we meet on the street corner we talk about the stray dog and wonder who owns it. He is a kind person who cares for both people and animals. This childlike man is as important as the mayor or any other city official.

The Bible tells us that if someone is so gifted that he or she can speak in other languages and yet cannot love, that person doesn't have much. People who love and show their love are the ones we should get to know.

"If I speak in the tongues of men and of angels, but have not love, I am only a resounding gong or a clanging cymbal" (1 Corinthians 13:1).

♦ ♦ ◆ ♦ ♦

Hate Groups

Everyone dislikes someone. It's hard to like everyone. But some people go out of their way to hate others. Some groups even meet regularly to discuss their hate for others. They may hate Jewish people or blacks or Catholics or Hispanics or someone else. You may have seen them on television. Maybe you have seen them in your city or neighborhood. We call them hate groups.

Members of hate groups might wear uniforms or hoods. They might carry weapons or burn crosses. Sometimes they are terribly frightening and they can be dangerous. Members of hate groups have killed people in the United States and in other countries.

Why do people join hate groups? Some want power. Some want to feel superior. Others like to scare people. A few join simply because they are lonely and want to belong to a group that accepts them. It's too bad that their group is centered on hating others. Most of us would rather join a group that serves and helps others rather than one that hates.

Often members of hate groups feel left out and afraid. I talked to three members of a hate group who had been to prison when they were younger. After their release they couldn't get jobs; they felt hopeless and were looking for purpose in life. They joined a group that welcomed them, but unfortunately it encouraged them to hate.

Members of hate groups like to blame their problems on others. Unwilling to take charge of their own lives and be responsible for themselves, they accuse a race or nationality or religion for their troubles.

People who are afraid and ignorant are likely to react the wrong way. Instead of trying to improve themselves they strike out to hurt someone else.

Hate groups are wrong. Hurting people is wrong. You should never participate in organizations that are prejudiced and cruel. You have no right to scribble on synagogue or church walls. You should never try to run people out of your neighborhood because of their race, religion, or nationality.

Jesus asks us to be accepting, loving, and tolerant of others. We don't have to be afraid and blame our problems on groups. Hate groups are not for followers of Jesus.

◆ ◆ ◆ ◆ ◆

Clothes Don't Count

Lindsay's parents didn't have much. Their house was neat but nothing fancy. She wore clean clothes but they weren't stylish. You never saw a brand name on her athletic shoes.

No one knew how Lindsay would have dressed if she had the money. But her friends never saw her wear anything expensive.

Because Lindsay didn't dress well, some of the children at school avoided her. They thought she must not be anything special or else she would wear better clothing.

Those who got to know her found out what a good friend she was. She was very creative and could have a good time without spending money. Lindsay had a great sense of humor and she was kind to everyone. If you forgot to bring your books home, you could call Lindsay and she would bring hers to your house to share. If you forgot your lunch money, she would be happy to split whatever money she had.

You could tell that she wasn't the kind of person who would talk about you. Lindsay didn't spread rumors and gossip about her friends.

She was a good person. Some people didn't like her because of her clothes. And some parents wouldn't let their children hang around her. Too bad, because those who got to know her found out what a great kid Lindsay was.

◆ ◆ ◆ ◆ ◆

People-Bashing

A family moved into a new neighborhood. They were a hardworking family with four children. The mother of the family was white and the father was black.

Soon after they moved into their home things were thrown at their house. Stones, eggs, garbage. People they had never met simply drove by and pelted their home with junk.

Soon their trash cans were set afire and windows were broken.

Some people hated the family merely because they were racially mixed. Although people had not even met the family, they hated them anyway.

Jesus would never want you to be part of people-bashing.

Two gay men walked down the street, minding their own business. A group of four young men began following them. As they moved along the sidewalk, one of the four men called one of the gay men a name. The word was a slur meant to insult him.

They all continued down the street for several blocks. The four young men picked up their pace, closing in on the two. As they walked, the name calling got louder and uglier. By now three of the four were shouting insults.

At the end of the fourth block, the two gay men suddenly turned and entered a restaurant. The four men slowed down and laughed, but fortunately they moved on.

Even if we don't agree with the way people live, we still have no right to harass and insult them. Jesus teaches us to love the people we don't agree with. We are never to be people-bashers.

At night in a large city, many street people look for some comfortable place to sleep. They collect old clothes and boxes to make temporary tents for the night. A torn coat may be their pillow and the pavement may be their bed.

It is hard to say why they have become street people. Their lives don't look like much fun and their future isn't bright.

Eventually everyone settles down and soon people are sleeping in alleys, beside heat grates, along the walls of buildings. The only sounds come from a few people snoring and an occasional car driving past.

Around 2:00 A.M., three men in their middle thirties appear on the street. As they walk along, they pull cardboard off the sleeping men, women, and children. They kick at the people's few belongings and call the half-asleep victims terrible names.

The trio of half-drunk troublemakers have no real purpose. They are out to cause mischief and make life miserable for others.

People can be cruel, especially to those who are less fortunate than themselves. Jesus asks us to act differently. We should love and help those who suffer. No one should be involved in people-bashing.

"Love your neighbor as yourself" (Matthew 22:39).

◆ ◆ ◆ ◆ ◆

Life Doesn't Stop
at Middle Age

When we are young we often think that everyone should be young. Young people like skateboards, shopping malls, shooting hoops, playing video games, and swimming. They enjoy loads of activities and lots of noise.

Many young people enjoy their own way of living and have little tolerance for those who are different. They don't have much patience for older people who might be slower, quieter, and have a few aches and pains.

The very word *old* is scary to many. And what is old? The age of thirty-five sounds "washed up" to someone who is twelve. When my father was forty, I wondered how he managed to keep going to work every day!

People who are older are often slower and sometimes quieter than children. However, some are very active. Many older people hike in the mountains, swim, go boating, learn new skills, and scuba dive. Others are less active but they care about others, read, visit, and tell great stories to children.

The temptation is to treat older people like a bunch of antiques. But they are important, and each one deserves respect and attention. Older people know things about sports, woodwork, people, and fun that young people will take years to learn.

"Rise in the presence of the aged, show respect for the elderly and revere your God. I am the Lord" (Leviticus 19:32).

Picked Last

Have you ever stood around while teams were being chosen? Maybe you were going to play basketball, soccer, baseball, or football. Each team's captain begins the selection process. The first person picked is probably the best athlete, then the second best and so on.

Aren't you relieved when you are finally chosen? It's no fun being the last person picked. You feel like a loser. You realize that you may not be the most coordinated person in the world, but you are willing to try hard. Maybe as you grow older your coordination will improve, and maybe not.

If you ever get to choose the teams, remember how painful it is to be picked last. Ask yourself this question: Why are you going to play this sport? Is it to have a good time or is it to beat the other team?

If you want to have a good time, there are better ways to pick people. Try one of these methods sometime:

1. Have everyone line up and count off by twos. The ones are one team and the twos are the other.
2. Put names in a hat and let each captain draw names.

Maybe you can invent a new system. But don't use a system where a certain boy or girl is always chosen last. If the goal is to have fun, then accept one another and allow everyone to feel welcome.

Children are hurt when they are always picked last. They feel left out and begin to feel bad about themselves. As Christians we should be more into encouragement and less into discouragement.

Jesus said the first will be last and the last will be first (Luke 13:30). Jesus wasn't talking about sports. He was referring to his kingdom. He was making a point about who and what are important.

The people we think of as important and gifted in this world may not be the same ones Jesus thinks are important. The person who is constantly picked last may have other talents that Jesus thinks are terrific!

When Jesus loves us he never asks first how well we hit a softball!

◆ ◆ ◆ ◆ ◆

Unemployed and Anxious

If your parents have jobs and go to work every day, you may wonder why other people don't do the same. Why do some adults hang around the house and not work for a living? Often we hear adults with jobs talk terribly about adults who don't have jobs.

Are people without jobs too lazy to work? Are they getting money from friends or relatives or the government while they refuse to get a job? Are the working people helping to pay for those who simply don't want to work?

Millions of adults don't have jobs. Some of them don't want to work. Some even work hard at avoiding work. But the majority of unemployed people would rather be working.

There are many reasons that people can't work. Some people get sick and can't go to work regularly. Factories sometimes lay off 1000, 2000 even 10,000 workers at one time. Those workers have trouble finding new jobs. In some areas of the country, laid-off workers look for a year or more for another place to work.

Everyone who can earn his or her own money should. The Bible tells us that. "If a man will not work he shall not eat" (2 Thessalonians 3:10). But millions of men and women simply cannot find a job. Should we be angry that they can live without working? Should we resent the fact that they receive food and money from the government in order to survive?

No. Jesus asks us to love one another. We should try to be understanding toward people who can't find jobs. All of us could be in that situation sometime in our lives. We should pay attention to our own lives and be sure we aren't doing anything to put down someone who is unemployed. Be slow to judge others and let God's love shine through you.

" 'Love the Lord your God with all your heart and with all your soul and with all your mind.' This is the first and greatest commandment. And the second is like it: 'Love your neighbor as yourself' " (Matthew 22:37-39).

◆ ◆ ◆ ◆ ◆

Strengths and Weaknesses

Each person seems to have some good qualities. No matter what someone's background, there are times when everyone is kind and considerate. There may be a few totally wicked people in the world, but not many.

But even the kindest person may act rude and insulting on a bad day. We are all a mix of good and evil, thoughtful and thoughtless.

I want others to be tolerant and understanding when I get short-tempered or inconsiderate. But I need to allow for the shortcomings of others, too. Everyone has weak moments, just as I have. We should never give up on an entire group of people simply because one member of that group acts rudely. We need to be accepting just as we want others to accept us.

When we wonder how to treat others, there is a great rule we can use. It's called the Golden Rule. The concept is that we should treat others in the same way we would like to be treated.

All of us want to be accepted in spite of our weaknesses. We need to accept others with their strengths and weaknesses too.

"In everything, do to others what you would have them do to you" (Matthew 7:12).

◆ ◆ ◆ ◆ ◆

Jesus above All

Sometime and somewhere, all of us will bow down in front of Jesus Christ: from the snow-covered Alps to the hot savannahs of Death Valley; from the busy streets of Buenos Aires to the quiet wilderness of Canada; from the rice paddies of China to the bush country of West Africa. People of all tribes and nations will meet at the feet of Christ.

When we meet together we will not be segregated. There won't be anyone with a microphone shouting out orders and directing groups. He won't be saying, "Now we want all the Chinese on the left. Let's have the Africans stand on the right. Now, you Europeans, we want you in the back."

When we meet together, our emphasis won't be on nationalities or race. Probably we won't even notice our differences. The feature of attraction will be Jesus Christ. His name will be more important than any other.

The prejudices that keep popping up their ugly heads in this life will all disappear. We will lay aside our differences and concentrate on one person, the Son of God.

But we don't have to wait until that day. We can start putting off our prejudices now because we already have Jesus to help us. Christ calls us to a life of servanthood and love, and the Holy Spirit helps guide us. We cannot stop hurtful thoughts and actions on our own. We need Jesus' saving love. How wonderful it will be when we bow down with people of all races and nationalities at the feet of Jesus Christ. And we can start now.

"Therefore God exalted him to the highest place and gave him the name that is above every name, that at the name of Jesus every knee should bow, in heaven and on earth and under the earth" (Philippians 2:9-10).